CONFERENCE
PROCEEDINGS

The United States, Europe, and the Wider Middle East

Shahram Chubin

Bruce Hoffman

William Rosenau

Supported by the Geneva Centre for Security Policy and
the RAND Center for Middle East Public Policy

T0308676

 RAND CENTER FOR MIDDLE EAST PUBLIC POLICY

The proceedings described here were supported by the RAND Center for Middle East Public Policy and the Geneva Centre for Security Policy.

ISBN 0-8330-3723-4

The RAND Corporation is a nonprofit research organization providing objective analysis and effective solutions that address the challenges facing the public and private sectors around the world. RAND's publications do not necessarily reflect the opinions of its research clients and sponsors.

RAND® is a registered trademark.

Published 2004 by the RAND Corporation
1776 Main Street, P.O. Box 2138, Santa Monica, CA 90407-2138
1200 South Hayes Street, Arlington, VA 22202-5050
201 North Craig Street, Suite 202, Pittsburgh, PA 15213-1516
RAND URL: http://www.rand.org/
To order RAND documents or to obtain additional information, contact
Distribution Services: Telephone: (310) 451-7002;
Fax: (310) 451-6915; Email: order@rand.org

Preface

On June 27–29, 2004, the Center for Middle East Public Policy (CMEPP), a RAND National Security Research Division program, and the Geneva Centre for Security Policy (GCSP) held a workshop focusing on the United States, Europe, and the greater Middle East. This conference was the fifth in a series of collaborative efforts by GCSP and RAND in the area of security policy. The GCSP and the CMEPP would like to thank William Rosenau for serving as the rapporteur for this meeting and all of the participants, who are listed in Appendix B.

The GCSP, an international foundation established in 1995, conducts training in international security policy for diplomats, military officers, and civil servants. The GCSP also carries out research to support these training activities, and holds conferences and seminars to promote dialogue on security-related issues. The Swiss government is the principal contributor to the GSCP budget.

For more on the center's research and training activities, please contact Shahram Chubin, the GCSP's head of academic affairs and director of research. He can be reached by email at s.chubin@gcsp.ch, by telephone at +41 22 906 16 00; or by mail at GCSP, Avenue de la Paix, 7bis, P.O. Box 1295, CH-1211 Geneva 1, Switzerland. Additional information on the GCSP is available at www.gcsp.ch.

The CMEPP is a center within the RAND National Security Research Division (NSRD). NSRD conducts research and analysis for the Office of the Secretary of Defense, the Joint Staff, the Unified Commands, the defense agencies, the Department of the Navy, the U.S. intelligence community, allied foreign governments and foundations. NSRD is a division of the RAND Corporation.

For more information about the CMEPP, please contact the director, David Aaron. He can be reached by email at David_Aaron@rand.org, by phone at +1 (310) 451-6997, extension 7782, or by mail at RAND Corporation, 1776 Main Street, P.O. Box 2138, Santa Monica, CA 90407-2138, USA. More information about RAND is available at www.rand.org.

Contents

The United States, Europe, and the Wider Middle East

Introduction

Middle East policy continues to be dominated by what one analyst has termed "the usual suspects," that is, the Israeli-Palestinian conflict, the proliferation of weapons of mass destruction (WMD), Iraq security, and other chronic security problems. At the same time, however, the region and, by extension, the United States and Europe face a variety of new policy challenges, including the spread of Islamist extremism, the growth of al-Qa'ida and affiliated groups, and the growing rift between the West and the wider Middle East.

This combination of new and perennial challenges served as the backdrop for an informal discussion among a group of experts who gathered to explore a set of five topics:

- the insurgency in Iraq
- the Arab-Israeli situation
- the terrorist threat
- internal security in Saudi Arabia
- Iran and the proliferation of WMD.

None of these issues was considered in isolation. Rather, each was addressed with an eye toward understanding their implications for the region as a whole and exploring what the broader consequences might be for American and European policy. The following summary reflects the rapporteur's sense of the conversation, which was conducted on a not-for-attribution basis.

Insurgency and Stabilization in Iraq

Given the dramatic nature of the ongoing violence in Iraq and the vast disparity between prewar American expectations and the reality of the occupation, it is hardly surprising that the insurgency has preoccupied policymakers, journalists, and analysts, including the participants at the conference. But for all this attention, the insurgency remains largely opaque. The United States and its coalition partners entered Iraq in March 2003 with little or no human intelligence and failed to develop reliable and productive human sources either during the major combat phase of operations or afterwards during the occupation. As a result, both the coalition military forces and the Coalition Provisional Authority were caught off guard when the insurgency emerged. Civilian police—an integral intelligence component in any counterinsurgency campaign—were not organized, trained, or equipped to provide human intelligence. The United States and its coalition partners failed to anticipate the outbreak of an insurgency, and when it did materialize, Washington and its allies ignored it. Today, the most basic questions about the guerrillas—such as their numbers, leadership (if any), and structure—remain unanswered. For example, are bombings, assassinations, and other insurgent attacks coordinated, thereby suggesting the emergence of a "central nervous system"; or does the existence of an obvious set of targets coupled with extensive media coverage obviate the need for a complex command-and-control structure? In addition, we know little about the role of neighboring powers such as Iran, which may be agitating Iraq's Shia population, and likely played a role in helping to transform the radical Shia cleric Moqtada al-Sadr into a popular leader. However, some experts note that Iran has no fundamental interest in promoting instability in Iraq, since such subversion would undercut the international good will it has worked long and hard to build. Rather, Iran's goal in Iraq is to ensure that whatever government emerges is neither a Western puppet nor an Islamic republic that might serve as a regional rival.

While much about the insurgency remains uncertain, several of the workshop participants were able to describe the contours of the uprising and suggest possible approaches for stabilizing the country, although few were optimistic about Iraq's security prospects, at least for the near and midterm. The groups fueling the instability are diverse. In addition to "fanatical holdouts" of the old regime, insurgents include

- criminal gangs, which are engaged in "industrial-scale" carjacking and housebreaking in cities such as Baghdad, Mosul, and Basra
- remnants of the Ba'ath regime's security services, who are reorganizing geographically and building networks based on personal relationships and loyalties
- Islamicized Iraqi nationalists, who have played a prominent role in recent political violence, such as the revolt in Fallujah
- foreign fighters, including al-Qa'ida and individuals and groups allegedly linked to it, such as Abu Musab al-Zarqawi and Ansar al-Islam.

Although each of these elements contributes to the insurgency, some are clearly more important than others. While the Coalition Provisional Authority has stressed the role of foreign jihadists, "former regime loyalists," and various "dead enders," the insurgency is undoubtedly a wider and more broad-based one composed of fighters from both the Sunni and Shia communities in Iraq. The collapse of public order and the security vacuum that followed the invasion and the destruction of the Ba'athist regime helped foster the insurgency and continue to sustain it. Iraqi society under Saddam Hussein was a highly militarized one, in which military training and automatic weapons were found widely among the population. Small arms and ammunition dumps scattered across the country allowed political and criminal elements ready access to weapons and ordnance. Nationalist and Islamist ideologies, long suppressed under the former regime, are enjoying a renaissance within the Iraqi polity, and are helping to fuel the movement resisting foreign and non-Muslim occupation.

Looking ahead, a few of the conference participants were guardedly optimistic about the short- and mid-term prospects for stabilizing Iraq, expressing some hope that society will self-stabilize. In their judgment, it will be particularly important to break the link between foreign jihadists who are pursuing a "scorched-earth" strategy and indigenous fighters who are seeking simply to control the state. However, most participants remained pessimistic about Iraq's future. Demobilizing insurgents will be a generations-long process. As the occupying forces struggle to reconstitute Iraq's police services, public safety remains nonexistent in much of the country, and criminals as well as political actors have exploited this law-and-order vacuum. Even if no one wants to see a civil war in Iraq, the volatile combination of militias, the lack of state authority and capacity, and ethnic tensions is a recipe for violent internal conflict, as it was in Lebanon during the 1970s. In classic totalitarian style, Saddam Hussein annihilated all aspects of indigenous civil society, thereby allowing him to atomize and then mobilize the population. Iraqis therefore are faced with the formidable challenge of building new institutions largely from scratch. Although the populace is among the most highly educated in the region, this offers no guarantee for future peace and stability, again as demonstrated in the case of Lebanon.

In addition to these daunting security challenges, Iraq also faces a potential economic and demographic crisis. Economic factors do not determine stability, but they do help to influence it. Iraq is heavily dependent on oil revenues, but this income is only sufficient for funding one-third of the country's national budget. State industries are utterly noncompetitive, but little economic reform is under way—for example, gasoline remains at the artificially low price of five cents per gallon. In all likelihood, Iraq will be under intense economic pressure, and the most the country can expect by 2013 is a per-capita income that is below that of Tunisia's today. The struggle for control of oil is another factor that could spark a civil war, as resource-oriented conflicts in sub-Saharan Africa have demonstrated during the last ten years.

Finally, the occupation of Iraq has helped widen the breach between much of the wider Middle East and the West, particularly the United States. The coalition's tribulations have helped create a festive mood among hard-core elements in the Arab world. Even among more moderate elements, the U.S. military's overreliance on firepower (such as the use of F-16s in Fallujah) has reinforced perceptions that the United States is interested solely in dominating Iraq and gaining access to its oil.

The Israeli-Palestinian Situation

While hardly the only problem in the region, the Israeli-Palestinian conflict is becoming a festering sore that no Arab state (and in fact, no Muslim state) can ignore. Within Israel, four main approaches to the conflict have emerged:

1. The "pure Sharonist" strategy, an essentially ideological and existential approach that holds that the conflict cannot be solved, but only managed, and "hard-core" issues such as Jerusalem and Palestinian refugees remain unsolved.
2. The "new solutions" school, which argues that since the preconditions for a general settlement no longer exist, and that a two-state solution is no longer applicable, fresh approaches are required.
3. The "Gaza optimists," who urge building on the opportunity created by the withdrawal, which they believe will have a ripple effect.
4. The "Gaza disaster" school, which holds that the withdrawal demonstrated that acts of terror pay in the end.

In the view of some of our participants, the Gaza optimists may ultimately be proved correct, since the disengagement together with the creation of the security fence could improve the chances for peace by calming Israeli fears of terrorism and demographic overrun. However, for most of our experts, the conflict appears to be essentially intractable. Although some 65 percent of Israelis and Palestinians favor a two-state, peaceful solution, a new ferocity has also emerged on both sides in which shooting rock throwers and attacking apartment houses have become routine tactics. For both parties, this has become an existential conflict in which they are fighting not simply to secure a more favorable bargaining position, but for their very survival. Little serious effort has been made to address the refugee question, and on the matter of Jerusalem, the fact that many Palestinians believe they hold the city in trust for all Muslims makes negotiation difficult if not impossible. The settlements are unpopular in Israel, but sympathizers are deeply entrenched in the bureaucracy, and settlers run roughshod over the government.

Adding to the air of gloom, several participants highlighted the fundamental problem of the lack of leadership—among the Palestinians, in Israel, and in the United States and Europe—and the continuing failure to build on the strong public support for a peaceful settlement. Given this absence of real leadership, it seems unlikely that popular suffering will abate. Participants also highlighted negative economic and demographic trends, a recurring theme throughout the conference. With the exception of natural gas, the West Bank and Gaza have no natural resources, making it nearly impossible to construct an economically viable state, and even if peace were to be achieved, the new state would remain an economic slum.

The Global Jihadist Dimension

Confronted by a massive post-9/11 counterterrorism mobilization and a global war on terrorism, al-Qa'ida has demonstrated resiliency and flexibility in adapting rapidly to the global war on terrorism. The loss of Afghanistan as a sanctuary and training ground appears to have had relatively little effect on al-Qa'ida's ability to stage significant terrorist operations, as demonstrated by subsequent attacks in Indonesia, Yemen, Morocco, Saudi Arabia, Kuwait, Kenya, Turkey, Spain, and elsewhere.

Indeed, in some respects, al-Qa'ida has been transformed into something potentially more threatening. No longer a unitary, hierarchical organization vulnerable to America's military power, al-Qa'ida has morphed into a globally distributed network with no clear center to attack. As a number of analysts have concluded, al-Qa'ida today is more akin to an ideology or global movement. Operating independently of Osama bin Laden but still inspired by his iconic status, "franchises" of affiliated groups wage the global jihad for the same broad set of objectives. Effective and persuasive al-Qa'ida propaganda, distributed directly through the Internet and indirectly via satellite channels like al-Jazeera, enables the al-Qa'ida message to penetrate deep into the Muslim world.

The United States and its partners have been able to kill or apprehend key figures like Khalid Sheik Mohammed, but al-Qa'ida has demonstrated a remarkable ability to replenish its mid-level cadres and keep its ranks filled with militants. Although the precise number of jihadists trained in the Afghan camps is uncertain, it is clear that many thousands received instruction in guerrilla warfare tactics, techniques, and procedures. While most of these individuals were not trained to conduct terrorist attacks, al-Qa'ida can nevertheless call on the services of jihadists positioned in some 60 countries around the world.

Al-Qa'ida also appears to retain access to sufficient funds to mount its operations, despite the significant progress that has been made in controlling terrorist fundraising and financial transactions. Since 9/11, cells have become increasingly self-sustaining, with funds generated through credit card fraud and other lucrative enterprises. The campaign to dry up terrorist financing has been hindered because terrorism is inherently low cost. For example, the October 2002 bombing in Bali, which killed 200 people and maimed hundreds more, cost under $35,000, according to one estimate.

It is remarkable that al-Qa'ida and its affiliates have been able to hold a steady strategic course in the face of an aggressive global counterterrorism campaign. That strategy, as articulated by bin Laden and his inner circle, identifies two principal targets: (1) The United States and the West (the so-called "far enemy") and (2) the "apostate" regimes that oppress Muslims in countries like Saudi Arabia, Egypt, and Pakistan (the "near enemy"). Although both target sets are critical, al-Qa'ida's operational focus has alternated back and forth between them, maintaining the flexibility to strike when vulnerabilities present fresh opportunities, as in Istanbul in November 2003.

Al-Qa'ida propaganda messages periodically reinforce the elements of this strategy and provide targeting guidance and operational instruction. The economic vulnerability of both sets of enemies has always been a prominent al-Qa'ida theme. The attacks on foreign workers in Saudi Arabia in the spring and summer of 2004 were intended to cripple the kingdom's economy by frightening off foreign investment. Similarly, in Iraq, targeting guidance conveyed through propaganda paved the way for a series of ferocious attacks on American, Korean, Turkish, and other foreign contractors.

Al-Qa'ida propagandists have long argued that guerrilla warfare is the most effective way for the weak to drive out the strong, as demonstrated in Afghanistan, Somalia, Algeria, and Vietnam. For al-Qa'ida, Iraq offers the promise of a Vietnam-style quagmire that saps the United States of manpower, treasure, and the political will to remain engaged in the region. While apparently unwilling to commit its most experienced fighters to Iraq, keeping the conflict simmering clearly serves a number of al-Qa'ida objectives—draining American strength, distracting the United States while al-Qa'ida and its affiliates strike elsewhere, and serving as a recruiting and propaganda tool for the global jihad.

As for the future, the conference participants agreed that countering the global threat posed by al-Qa'ida in Iraq and elsewhere will require new approaches. First, counterterrorism policy and operations must be flexible enough to adjust to al-Qa'ida's fluid strategy. Second, the United States must counter the perception of America as a sinister force intent on destroying Islam and enriching itself at the expense of the Muslim world. Unlike the traditional European terrorist groups of the 1970s and 1980s, such as the Red Army Faction and the Red Brigades, al-Qa'ida has become a mass-based movement. Al-Jazeera and other electronic media in the Muslim world are increasingly important sources of information, and it is essential that American officials stop shunning these powerful media outlets and learn how to employ them more effectively to counter misinformation and misperceptions. Finally, the United States should abandon the concept of a "war on terrorism" and develop a clearer strategy for countering the threat posed by al-Qa'ida.

Saudi Arabia

The last several years have not been particularly bright ones for the kingdom. The 9/11 attacks led to widespread criticism of Saudi Arabia in the United States, its closest ally. Critics attacked the kingdom's global campaign to promote Wahhabism, its alleged support for the 9/11 hijackers, and its treatment of women and religious minorities. Many of Saudi Arabia's financial, educational, and social institutions were condemned as fundamentally illegitimate. The kingdom's inability to side openly with the United States over Iraq added to the deterioration of the relationship.

Some of the conference participants suggested that the wave of terrorist violence in 2004 marked the emergence of a full-blown insurgency inside Saudi Arabia, and in their view, the violence highlights three particular causes for concern: (1) the loyalty and efficacy of the security forces, (2) the apparent failure of the tried-and-true methods of co-opting internal adversaries, and (3) the fragmentation of religious and monarchical authority. For other participants, however, the Saudi security situation appeared less bleak; they noted that predictions about the kingdom's demise are long-standing. While these participants acknowledged that jihadists enjoy popular support, they believe it is also clear that most Saudis lack any real political consciousness and tend to reflexively back the royal family. In addition, it is a mistake to lump all of the security forces together. The local police, to be sure, are deeply divided and not particularly competent, but they are relatively unimportant with respect to internal security. For defeating a subversive movement, the essential forces are the security services, which are controlled by the interior ministry. Although it is difficult to assess their capabilities, there is no firm evidence that they have collaborated with the regime's violent adversaries, and what is more, low-level penetration is a fact of life in all security services, including the Central Intelligence Agency and the Federal Bureau of Investigation.

Iran and WMD

Within Iran, advocates of "going nuclear" are not limited to the mullahs, but include a variety of nationalist elements. In the view of these advocates, Iran has been unfairly pressured to forgo technological weapons that the country has every legitimate right to pursue. Moreover, some conference participants argued, Iran has aspirations to be recognized as a regional superpower and may consider it necessary to have a hedge and/or option in a region of simmering tensions and several nuclear powers, both of which contribute to a nuclear imperative. Acquiring a nuclear arsenal might also enable Teheran to resist Western pressure for democratization and, by "playing the nationalist card," legitimize the regime domestically.

That said, there are openings that the United States could exploit. The regime is on a quest for legitimacy and has long had a fixation on reestablishing ties with the United States. Teheran perceives improved relations with the United States as one way of addressing pressing internal economic and demographic challenges, including the formidable necessity to create 300,000 new jobs every year. These pressures, combined with the search for legitimacy, might make Teheran more willing than in the past to strike a deal with Washington.

Ultimately, the only long-term solution to the problem posed by potential Iranian nuclear proliferation is for a democratic political order to emerge. A democratic Iran would have less of an existential necessity for developing nuclear weapons, as several of the conference participants noted. Today the democratic movement is in tactical retreat, but a debate over nuclear weapons could help revive mass-based support for a freer political order. The Iranian people, who have been excluded from the regime's deliberations, might provide real political pressure once the true economic and security costs of a nuclear weapons program become more widely known.

Concluding Observations

Throughout the conference, the participants, in addition to considering urgent immediate issues like the insurgency in Iraq, addressed underlying economic, demographic, and political developments that have important implications for the wider Middle East and the region's relations with the West. When oil is factored out, the region has been in steady economic decline for the last 50 years, and there are few obvious prospects for reversing this trend. With women economically marginalized, half of the region's human capital is largely unavailable for economically productive uses. During this period, the population has moved from rural to urban to "hyper-urban" settings, and there is little understanding of how this movement has contributed to social challenges or the emergence of radicalism. All of the countries in the region face the problem of how to employ university graduates, many of whom have received substandard educations.

Across the region, there is a growing popular sense of despair, as reflected in a recent poll in which 50 percent of the respondents identified "migration" as their principal career objective. A backbone of resentment runs through these societies, whose populations have become more urban, more political, and more easily mobilized. As noted by several of the participants, countries like Egypt, Saudi Arabia, Iran, Algeria, and Morocco have become stagnant, fragmented, and self-pitying. Each of these countries is made up of three parts: At the top, in the "palace," a tiny group of rulers seeks closer ties with the West; in the basement, an equally small group of fanatics builds bombs and plots destruction; and finally, out in the street, society's vast middle languishes.

As for the future, it seems certain that the United States and Europe will continue to be engaged in the region, and at the same time, the West will continue to be resented. It is regrettable that the United States and Europe have done little to engage home-grown groups that are promoting democracy, transparency, and a freer political, economic, and social order, and for the time being, at least, the West—and in particular, the United States—will continue to be seen as the principal problem in the eyes of the Arab world.

Conference Schedule

The United States, Europe, and the Wider Middle East
GCSP/RAND Annual Conference
Geneva, June 27–29, 2004

Sunday, 27 June 2004

19h30   Dinner at the Hôtel d'Angleterre

               Keynote Address: Iraq and After
               Dr. Anthony H. Cordesman, Arleigh A. Burke Chair in Strategy, Middle East Studies Program, Center for Strategic and International Studies, Washington, D.C.

Monday, 28 June 2004

09h00–09h15   **Welcome and Introduction**
               Dr. Shahram Chubin, Director of Research, GCSP

               Dr. Bruce Hoffman, Acting Director, Center for Middle East Public Policy, RAND

09h15–10h45   **Iraq: Stabilization and Extrication**
               Chair: Ambassador James Dobbins, Director, International Security and Defense Policy Center, RAND

               Speaker: Dr. Toby Dodge, Senior Fellow, Economic and Social Research Council, Centre for the Study of Globalisation and Regionalisation, University of Warwick and Consulting Senior Fellow for the Middle East, IISS, London

10h45–11h15   *Coffee Break*

11h15–12h00   **General Discussion**

12h00–13h00	*Buffet Lunch*

13h00–15h00	**Iraq and Its Neighbors** Chair: Ambassador James Dobbins, Director, International Security and Defense Policy Center, RAND

Syria

Dr. Volker Perthes, Stiftung Wissenschaft und Politik (SW), Berlin

Saudi Arabia

Dr. Ibrahim Karawan, Director, Middle East Center, University of Utah
Dr. Joshua Teitelbaum, Senior Research Fellow, Moshe Dayan Center for Middle Eastern and African Studies, Tel Aviv University

Turkey

Dr. Philip J. Robins, Lecturer in the Politics of the Middle East, St. Antony's College, University of Oxford

The GCC

Mr. Abdullah Alshayeji, Political Science Professor, Kuwait University

15h00–15h30	*Coffee Break*
15h30–17h00	**General Discussion**
19h30	*Dinner at Chez Jacky*

Tuesday, 29 June 2004

09h00–10h30	**Discussion on the Arab-Israeli Situation** Chair: Dr. Bruce Hoffman, Acting Director, Center for Middle East Public Policy, RAND

Dr. Alain Dieckhoff, Research Director, Center for International Studies and Research (CERI), Paris

Dr. Ahmad Khalidi, Senior Associate Member, St. Antony's College, Oxford University

Mr. Rami Khouri, Executive Editor, *Daily Star,* Beirut

Dr. Joshua Teitelbaum, Research Fellow, Moshe Dayan Center for Middle Eastern and African Studies, Tel Aviv University

10h30–11h00	*Coffee Break*

11h00–12h30   **The Jihadist, Terrorist Dimension**
Chair: Mr. Rami Khouri, Executive Editor, *Daily Star,* Beirut

Speaker: Dr. Bruce Hoffman, Acting Director, Center for Middle East Public Policy, RAND

Dr. William Rosenau, Political Scientist, RAND

12h30–13h30	*Buffet Lunch*

13h30–15h00   **Iran and Proliferation of WMD**
Chair: Dr. Shahram Chubin, Director of Research, GCSP

Prof. Abbas Milani, Visiting Professor of Political Science and Fellow, Hoover Institution, Stanford University

15h00–15h30	*Coffee Break*

15h30–17h00   **The US, Europe, and the Wider Middle East**
Chair: Prof. Michael A. McFaul, Senior Associate, Carnegie Endowment for International Peace and Associate Professor of Political Science, Hoover Institution, Stanford University

Dr. Anthony H. Cordesman, Arleigh A. Burke Chair in Strategy, Middle East Studies Program, Center for Strategic and International Studies, Washington, D.C.

Dr. James Dobbins, Director, International Security and Defense Policy Center, RAND

Mr. Rami Khouri, Executive Editor, *Daily Star,* Beirut

Dr. Ibrahim Karawan, Director, Middle East Center, University of Utah

19h30	*Concluding Dinner at Brasserie Lipp*

Conference Participants

Abdullah Alshayeji, Political Science Professor, Kuwait University

Esmail Amid-Hozour, Eton Corporation, Palo Alto, USA

Shahram Chubin, Director of Research, GCSP

Anthony H. Cordesman, Arleigh A. Burke Chair in Strategy, Middle East Studies Program, Center for Strategic and International Studies, Washington, D.C.

Alain Dieckhoff, Research Director, Center for International Studies and Research (CERI), Paris

James Dobbins, Director, International Security and Defense Policy Center, RAND Corporation

Toby Dodge, Senior Fellow, Economic and Social Research Council, Centre for the Study of Globalisation and Regionalisation, University of Warwick, and Consulting Senior Fellow for the Middle East, IISS, London

Bruce Hoffman, Acting Director, Center for Middle East Public Policy, RAND

Ibrahim Karawan, Director, Middle East Center, University of Utah

Ahmad Khalidi, Senior Associate Member, St. Antony's College, Oxford University

Rami Khouri, Executive Editor, *Daily Star,* Beirut

Michael A. McFaul, Senior Associate, Carnegie Endowment for International Peace and Associate Professor of Political Science, Hoover Institution, Stanford University

Abbas Milani, Visiting Professor of Political Science and Fellow, Hoover Institution, Stanford University

Volker Perthes, Stiftung Wissenschaft und Politik (SWP), Berlin, Germany

Philip J. Robins, Lecturer in the Politics of the Middle East, St. Antony's College, University of Oxford

William Rosenau, Political Scientist, RAND Corporation

Joshua Teitelbaum, Senior Research Fellow, Moshe Dayan Center for Middle Eastern and African Studies, Tel Aviv University